P9-DDF-127

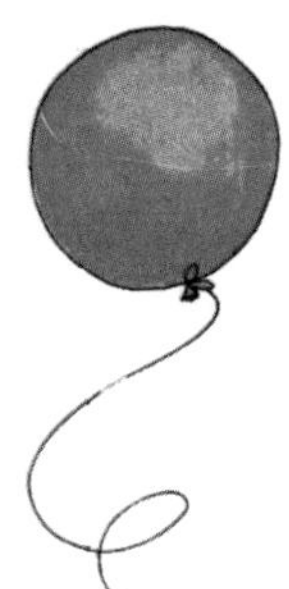

Presented To:

Date:

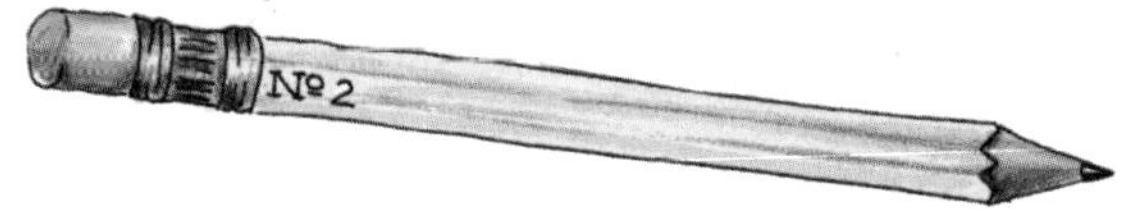

Dedication:

To Barbara and Steve:
Thank you for sharing what you're learning on your journey of faith.

Blessings,
Carolyn Larsen

for

Mothers & Daughters

Produced by Educational Publishing Concepts, Inc. Wheaton, Illinois.
Published by New Kids Media™ in association with Baker Book House
Company, P.O. Box 6287 Grand Rapids, Michigan 49516-6287.

ISBN 0-8010-4422 7

Printed in the United States of America.

2 3 4 5 6 7 — 02 01 00 99

for

Mothers & Daughters

Carolyn Larsen

Illustrated by Caron Turk

Published in association with

Dear Moms,

What a privilege it is to encourage your little girls to make prayer a daily part of their lives. Caron and I hope that *The Little Girls Book of Prayers* will help your little girls learn that they can talk to God about anything and everything.

The prayers in this book are loosely divided into the four forms that prayer takes: Adoration, Confession, Thanksgiving, and Supplication. As you read through these prayers with your little girl, I encourage you to personalize them—think of things that your little girl adores about God; or things she may need to confess. Help her express to God things that she is thankful for and discuss needs she has or those of people she cares about and bring those to God.

Caron Turk has again created delightful illustrations and has hidden a little angel with pink dotted wings in every one. Have fun looking for her!

Caron and I pray that this book of prayers will be a blessing to you and your little girl and that it will begin a lifelong habit of daily prayer for your little girl.

Blessings!
Carolyn Larsen

Contents

Dear God,

You love me! I know that you do 'cause the Bible tells me so. Sometimes when I'm having a bad day it makes me feel better just to remember that you love me! That makes me feel pretty special. Thank you, God and guess what? I love you, too!

Amen

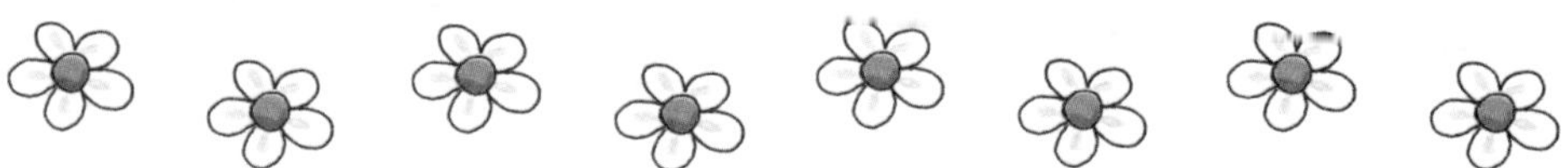

BIBLE
God loves me ... this I know... the Bible tells me so.

Dear God,

Sometimes when I'm trying to learn something new I need extra-special help. I get discouraged when something is hard to learn. I know I can ask for your help anytime because you care about everything that happens to me! Thank you for helping me whenever I ask.

Amen

God, help me..

Dear God,

Wow! When I watch the lightning flash in a thunderstorm or a waterfall splashing down, I see how strong and mighty you are. You are so strong, I know you can help me with any troubles I have! Nothing is too hard for you!

Amen

Gods strength is awesome!

Dear God,

When I'm having a happy day, I want to tell you about it. When I'm having a sad day, I want to tell you about it. That's 'cause I know you care about me no matter what. Thank you for caring about my happy times and my sad times, too.

Amen

Dear God,

Was it fun to make the world? Did it tickle when you made feathers? How did you think of jellyfish? Where did you get the idea for snapdragons? How come people come in so many different shapes and sizes? You had a zillion ideas and it's fun to look at everything you made. One of my favorite things is watching the sky turn orange, pink and purple when the sun goes to bed. You sure made neat things for us!

Amen

YoYo
GOD LOVES fish....
FISH
MY DOG
Jesus Loves me

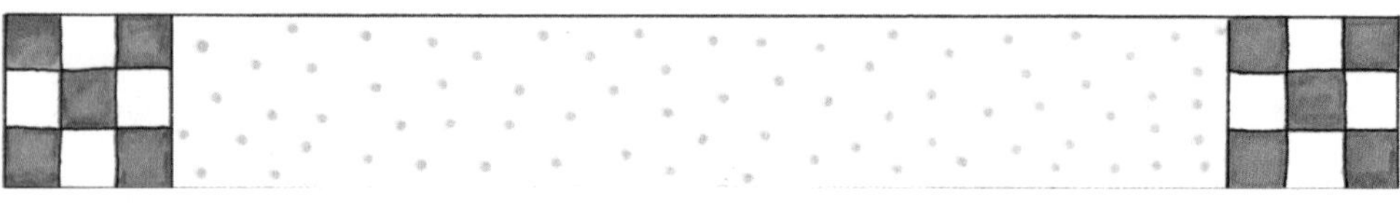

Dear Father,

Is there anything that you can't do? I don't think so. You put the stars in the sky and told them just where to stay. You made the earth circle around and around the sun. Then you made dandelion fuzzies and pretty flowers that grow right up through rocks. I'm pretty sure you can do anything!

Amen

God can do anything

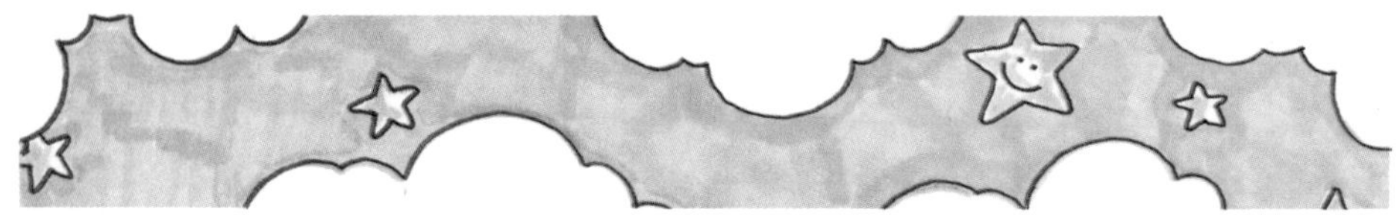

Dear God,

Thank you for being the same every single day. I don't have to wonder if you're having a bad day or a good day. I can talk to you when I feel mad or sad or happy. I can tell you if I'm grumpy or disappointed. Thank you that you love me no matter what!

Amen

"Thank you"

Dear Father,

Today I just feel happy. When I look at the trees I'm happy, when my puppy licks my face I'm happy. I just want to hug everyone I see. In fact, I'd like to hug you, God, 'cause you are the reason I feel so happy. Thank you, God, thank you for everything!

Amen

Thank You
God

Dear God,

Know what? I love you! I love you for all the wonderful things you do for me every day and for all the great things you give me every day. I love you for being so strong and powerful and gentle and kind. You are so awesome!

Amen

God
is
Awesome

Dear God,

Do you get tired? You must be busy all the time doing stuff for people and listening to our prayers. Do you ever want to take a nap or just stop doing things? I'm glad you don't 'cause we need you all the time.

Amen

I Wonder?
z z z
z z z

Dear God,

Did you know that I think about you sometimes even when I'm not in church or Mommy and Daddy aren't praying with me? I like to think about you 'cause it makes me feel good.

Amen

I feel good when
I think about God!

Dear God,

You know that story of Jairus' little girl who was really sick, then she died but Jesus made her alive again? That's a good story.

Amen

...This is a good story...

Dear God,

I did something wrong and I'm sorry. I cheated when I was playing a game with my friend. I just wanted to win the game, but it was wrong to cheat. I told my friend that I'm sorry, and I want to tell you, too. Please forgive me and help me to not cheat anymore. Thank you.

Amen

GAME RULES
God will forgive you

Dear God,

Sometimes my brother makes me so mad. It feels like he always gets his way and that Mom takes his side against me. When I got mad at him this afternoon I hit him and kicked down the blocks he was playing with. I'm sorry. I shouldn't have lost my temper. Please forgive me, and help me to be nicer to my brother, even when it's hard.

Amen

Dear Father,

My mom says she doesn't always like the things I do, but she always loves me. Well, today I did something she really didn't like. Mom asked me to clean my room. But, I just pushed everything into the closet and shut the door and told Mom that I was finished. I disobeyed AND I lied. I've had a crummy day just 'cause I feel so bad. I'm really sorry. Mom forgave me, will you please forgive me, too?

Amen

Bless This Mess
Love
My Stuff

Dear God,

I wish I could take back the mean words I said. I didn't really mean them. I know they made my friend feel bad 'cause her face looked really sad, even when I said I was sorry. Help my friend to forgive me and please help me to not say mean things anymore.

Amen

Dear God,
I made my
friend feel
bad. I'm so
sorry. I hop
you will forgiv
me. I Love
You.

Dear God,

I feel ugly inside because I took something that belongs to my friend. I've always liked her pretty gold bracelet. Today it was laying on the table so I just put it in my pocket. No one knows—except me and you. I'm really sorry. I don't like the way I feel. I'm going to take it back to my friend and ask her to forgive me. I hope she will. I want you to forgive me, too.

Amen

God will forgive you

Dear Father,

Today some kids on the playground were saying bad things about another girl so I did, too. Other people are going to think bad things about her because of what I said. I'm really sorry. Next time please help me to be strong and not say bad things. Please forgive me.

Amen

They aren't very nice...

Dear Father,

I feel crummy because I broke a promise I made to my mom. I promised her I would clean my room but I didn't do it. When I make a promise to Mom she trusts me to keep it. Now it will be harder for her to trust my promises. I'm really sorry. I hope she will forgive me. Will you forgive me, too?

Amen

Dear Mom,
I am sorry
I broke my
promise to you.
I will try harder.
I pray God will help
me to keep

Dear God,

Mom says that nothing should ever be more important to me than you are. I try to be sure that you are most important but sometimes I guess Mom and Dad are more important to me. I love you, but Mom and Dad have skin on and they can give me real live hugs. I know it's OK to love my mom and dad, but please help me to love you more!

Amen

Thank you God for my mom and dad.

Dear Father,

Some people I know say your name when they are angry; like it is a bad word. One of the Ten Commandments says not to do that so I know it's wrong. I am really sorry that I used your name like that, too. I didn't mean to, it just slipped out—I guess because I heard other people saying it. I'm really sorry, will you please forgive me? Help me to be strong enough to never do that again.

Amen

Commandment
3...
Do not use
God's name in
anger

Dear God,

Wow are you patient! I don't mean to but I keep making the same mistakes over and over. You forgive me every time I ask. I'm sorry that I'm so slow in learning things, I don't mean to be. Mom says not to get discouraged 'cause I'm still learning how to be a people. Thank you for being patient with me.

Amen

Thank you for your patience!

Dear God,

Know what I need help with? Obeying. It's hard because it seems like there is always someone telling me to do something and . . . well, I get tired of obeying. Please help me to be better at obeying.

Amen

Please feed the cat!
Go do your homework.
Be nice to your brother

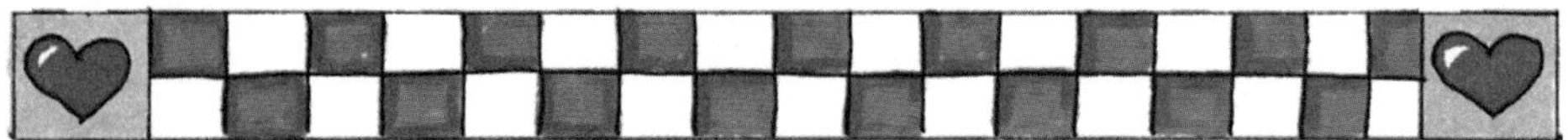

Dear God,

I have the best mom in the whole world. She reads with me and sings funny songs and plays soccer in the back yard. You knew just what kind of mom would be the best mom for me.

Someday when I'm a mom I hope I can be just like her. Thank you, God, for my mom.

Amen

I have the best mom in the world...
Read
STORY TIME
XOXO

Dear Father,

Thank you for my daddy. He loves me a lot. Sometimes Daddy picks me up and we dance all around the room singing at the top of our lungs. I especially like when Daddy and Mommy tuck me in bed and listen to my prayers. Daddy works hard but he still has time to play with me. I love my daddy. I'm glad that you love him, too.

Amen

I love my daddy ♥ He loves me alot ♥ We dance all around the room ♥ we like to sing ♥ We like to laugh ♥

Dear God,

Yippee! It's Saturday so there's no school! Thank you for days off when I can sleep late and then do fun "Saturday things." It's nice to have time to play with my friends or have picnics with my family. Thank you, God, for Saturdays.

Amen

God Loves me
Treasures
CRAFTS

Dear God,

I have the greatest family! Thank you for them. Sometimes I fight with my brothers and sisters, and I don't always obey Mom and Dad, but I really love them all. I know they love me, too. Help me show them how much I love them by the way I treat them.

Amen

My
Family

Dear God,

I love pets! I love my puppy's kisses and he makes me laugh when he chases his tail. It's so fun to watch my kitten when she sleeps in all sorts of strange positions. My friend and I sit and watch her iguana, Audree, 'cause it's very big and it sits very still, hardly moving for the whole day! Pets of all kinds are fun to play with or talk to, or just to sit and watch. Thank you, God, for pets.

Amen

Audree

Dear God,

Snow! I love it. It tickles when it falls on my face and it is so much fun catching snowflakes on my tongue, and making snowangels with my friends, and building snowmen families with my dad, and watching the snowflakes twinkle in the moonlight. Thank you, God, for thinking of snow. What a great idea!

Amen

Snow Angel

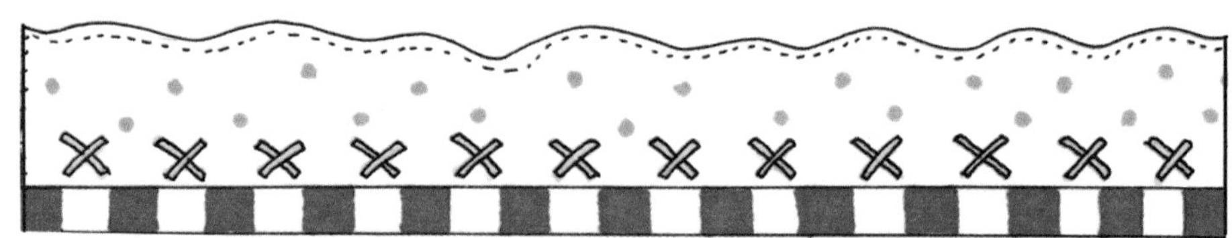

Dear God,

Thank you for sending Jesus to die for my sins. You must really love me lots to let your own Son come to earth for me. Some people weren't very nice to him and that must have made you sad. Thank you that you and Jesus cared enough about people to come up with a great plan so we can be in heaven with you someday.

Amen

LOVE
The Bible
Jesus Loves me

Dear God,

My grandma and grandpa are the greatest. I love them so much. I'm so glad that they love you. I learn more about you by watching the way they live. Thanks for thinking about how much fun it would be for kids to know their mom and dad's parents. I like hearing the stories Grandma and Grandpa tell about when Mom was a little girl. Thank you so much for my grandma and grandpa.

Amen

Dear God,

School is so much fun! Thank you for my teacher. She works hard to make our lessons fun and interesting. Thank you that she notices when someone in the class is lonely or sad. Thank you that she makes us laugh sometimes and tells us funny stories. Keep giving her good ideas, God!

Amen

№ 2
Good Morning
count
123456
PEACE
Around the World
FOOD
FISH
A+
Teacher
MATH

Dear God,

Thank you for friends. Anything I do is so much more fun when I do it with a friend. My friends cheer me up when I'm sad and laugh with me when I'm happy. Thank you that even if I mess up or am mean to my friends, they forgive me. Thank you for my friends—they are the best!

Amen

Girl Friends

Dear God,

It's my birthday! Thank you for making me and for putting me in my family. Thank you for birthday parties and birthday cake and for people who love me and make my special days even more special! Thank you, God, for birthdays.

Amen

HAPPY BIRTHDAY
B
Birthday
Girl

Dear Father,

My favorite Sunday of the whole year is Easter Sunday. Thank you that Jesus came to die for my sins. And thank you for bringing him back to life on that first Easter! I'm so happy to know that Jesus is alive right now and that he loves me. I love Jesus, too!

Amen

Happy Easter
Jesus is Alive!

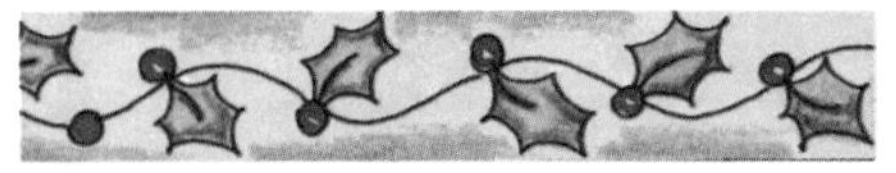
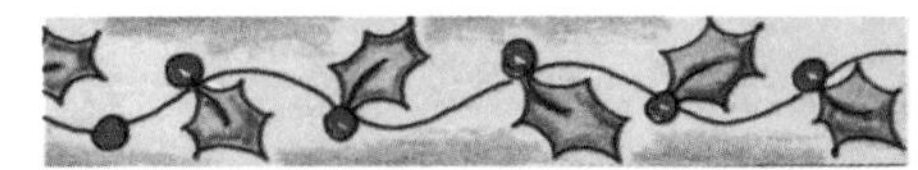

Dear God,

I know that you love me a lot because you let your son, Jesus come live on earth as a human being. That first Christmas, when Jesus was born, must have been so awesome. I love Christmas carols, and decorating the tree, and wrapping presents. Thank you, God, for Christmas!

Amen

Dear Father,

Yum! I love Thanksgiving! My aunts and uncles come and we have a big dinner, then I play with my cousins. The house smells good on Thanksgiving morning and all the food tastes so yummy (except for the mashed rutabaga—yuk). My favorite time is right before dinner when Daddy asks us to say something we are thankful for. Thank you for a special day to say thank you for everything you give us!

Amen

Be Thankful
God bless this meal

Dear God,

Happy New Year! We have a brand new calendar and a brand new year number to remember. Momma says a new year means I will have another birthday, and another Christmas, and another Easter ...everything! Thank you for the new year and thank you that we get to do everything again!

Amen

HAPPY NEW YEAR
JANUARY
FEBRUARY
MARCH
APRIL
MAY
JUNE
JULY
AUGUST
SEPTEMBER
OCTOBER
NOVEMBER
DECEMBER

Dear God,

Clouds are so awesome. Sometimes they look soft and fluffy—like they would be fun to jump around on. Sometimes they look big and angry. I like to lie on the ground and watch the pictures clouds make in the sky. Clouds always remind me of you. Thank you for clouds.

Amen

Dear God,

Thank you for my minister. He works really hard at our church but he still takes time to be nice to kids. Thank you for helping him preach good sermons, even if I don't always understand the big words he uses. Thank you that he loves you and teaches us to love you, too.

Amen

Dear Father,

Sunshine is awesome! I love the way it feels warm on my skin. Everything looks so bright and colorful when the sun is shining. Even on days when I feel sad everything seems better because the sun is shining. Thank you for sunshine.

Amen

Here comes the Sun.....

Dear Father,

It's rainy today. Sometimes I don't like rain. But, today Mommy let me put on my raincoat and boots and play in the rain. My friend and I splashed and jumped in the puddles. Then we floated leaf boats in the puddles. It was fun. Thank you for rain.

Amen

Dear God,

What a good idea you had to make flowers. You must like pretty colors and nice smells. Does that mean there are flowers in heaven? Flowers help us remember that someone loves us when we're sad and make us feel special when we're happy. Thank you for flowers.

Amen

Dear God,

Summer is over and that's sad. But, a good thing is that it's very pretty outside. The leaves have turned to yellow, orange and red and the sky is really blue. It kind of looks like everything is going to sleep for the winter. Thank you for autumn and for taking care of the trees and grass during the cold cold winter!

Amen

W N
S E
Autumn

Dear God,

Yahoo! Our family is going on vacation. For one whole week Mom and Dad don't have to go to work. We can play on the beach and stay up late and sleep in and forget about our chores at home. I love being with my family. Help us to have a great time together!

Thank you for vacations, God.

Amen

SKI
E-Z
TENT
VACATION
BOUND
Vacation
Fun
Beach
Relax
Adventure

Dear God,

Hey, I'm getting bigger. My clothes don't fit too good anymore. My muscles are getting stronger, and I feel really good. I guess I don't usually remember to thank you that I am healthy. But, I'm thanking you now. Thank you for keeping me healthy. Thank you for helping my body grow bigger and stronger.

Amen

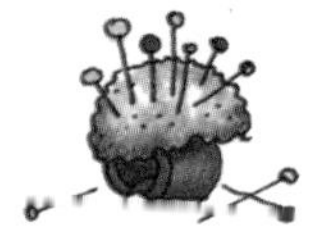

Dear God,

Thank you that I can go to school. I don't always want to go and I don't always want to learn. But, I'm really glad there is a place where I can learn new things. It's fun to be with my friends and the teacher makes learning fun. Kids in some places don't have a school to go to, so I just want to thank you for my school.

Amen

Aa Bb Cc Dd Ee Ff
Gg Hh Ii Jj Kk Ll Mm
Nn Oo Pp Qq Rr Ss
Tt Uu Vv Ww Xx Yy Zz
SCHOOL
Welcome
STOP

Dear God,

Today I saw a whole rainbow. When you made rainbows, did you know how much fun it would be for us to look at them? Rainbows are so pretty and they remind me that you keep your promises, just like in the story of Noah's ark. Thank you for rainbows!

Amen

God's promise
Glue

Dear God,

I'm so excited! I prayed and asked you for something—and it happened! It's so cool to know that you are listening and that you care about the things that are important to me. You can do anything in the whole world! Thank you for answering my prayers.

Amen

Bible

Dear Lord,

I love peanut butter and jelly sandwiches! Thank you for food. I always have enough to eat and sometimes I forget that there are kids who don't have enough. Thank you for apples and cupcakes and pizza and hamburgers (but you could have skipped brussels sprouts).

Amen

Grandmas
Jelly

Dear God,

You must really love me! Thank you for planning a way that I can come to heaven to be with you someday. Thank you that Jesus died for my sins and that you brought him back to life. I'm glad to know that when I die I can be in heaven with you—forever!

Amen

Thank you
God for
sending your
Son to die
for me. No
I can g
to heave

Dear God,

It's cold and rainy and yucky outside. I'm really glad that I have a warm, dry home to be in. Thank you for my home and for my warm soft bed and electric lamps to light my room and our kitchen that smells like yummy food. Thank you for everything you've given me.

Amen

Dear God,

Thank you for the Bible. Did you know that we would like to read about people who loved you—even people who knew Jesus personally? It's so cool to read about the miracles you did for your people and the way that you guided them. When I read those stories it helps me know that you will take care of me, too.

Amen

Jesus said to
be still. Then he
told the wind
stop blowing
sea began
Jesus and His Friends
Angels

Dear God,

I like to read about Noah and Moses and King David and other people who loved you. It's exciting to read what happened to them and how they had to go through some hard things, but you kept helping them and you never left them alone. Thank you for having someone write down those stories.

Amen

Exciting People in the Bible...
Noah
Moses
King David
and
many ♥ more...
ADVENTURE IN BIBLE STORIES

Dear Lord,

I think you must like music 'cause you made so many different kinds. I like loud happy music that makes my toes bounce up and down. When I sing at the top of my lungs about how much you love me Mommy says I am making a joyful noise! I think there will be music all the time in heaven!

Amen

...a joyful noise......

Dear God,

Thank you for my country. Sometimes I hear on the news about countries where the people can't go to church or pray to you. Thank you for the freedom we have here. Please help the people who run our country. Help them to make good decisions, and to always talk to you before they make them.

Amen

God Bless Our Country

Dear Father,

Thank you for my doctor She went to school for a long, long time to learn how to take care of me and know when something is wrong. She is so nice and gentle that it's not even scary when I have to go see her. I know she can take care of me no matter what!

Amen

God
Bless th
Children
of the
World

Dear God,

We got report cards today. Sometimes that's a scary thing but most of the time I'm glad to see how I'm doing in my classes—and glad for my parents to see, too. Sometimes my teacher writes nice notes on my report, too. Thank you for report cards—wow, I didn't think I'd ever say that.

Amen

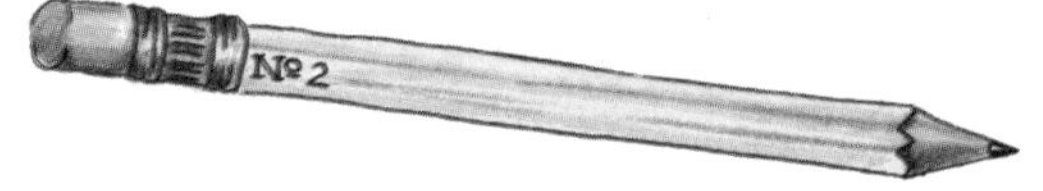

№ 2
Great Job!
REPORT CARD
Grade
Subject
Comments
B+
ENGLISH
A
HISTORY
A-
MATH
B
SCIENCE
Good to have in class
Excellent student
pleasure to have in class
Enthusiastic! Joyful
A NOTE FROM TEACHER
Great Job!
All your hard work has paid off.
I'm proud of You!
Mrs. Andrews

Dear Lord,

I love my church. It's so cool that I can go there and learn about you and sing songs about how much I love you. I have good friends at church and I know they care about me. I love being with other people who love you! Thank you for my church!

Amen

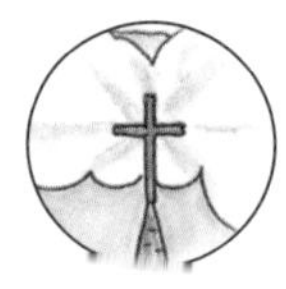

Dear God,

I like the story of how little David beat big ol' Goliath. Being little is not always a bad thing . . . especially if the little person loves you. Thanks for putting the David story in the Bible.

Amen

..Being little is not always a bad thing...

Dear God,

There must be a zillion stars out tonight. They are so pretty and the sky would just be black nothing without them. Was it fun to toss them out and see where they landed? I sure like looking at them. Thank you for stars.

Amen

Dear God,

How did you think of making the sky blue and the grass green? You could have made the sky purple and the grass pink. That would look funny. Thank you for making everything exactly right.

Amen

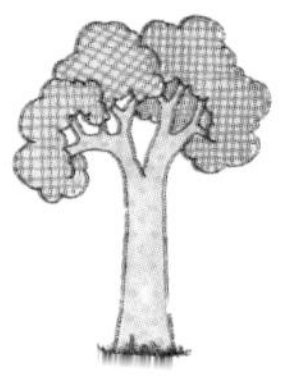

Dear Father,

My mom and dad are so much fun. Sometimes we go fishing, sometimes we bake cookies, sometimes we get ice cream. I just like to be with Mom and Dad. Thanks for the fun times we have.

Amen

UGAR
Sugar Cookies
1 c. sugar
1 c. flour
TTER COOKIES
COOKIES baked with love

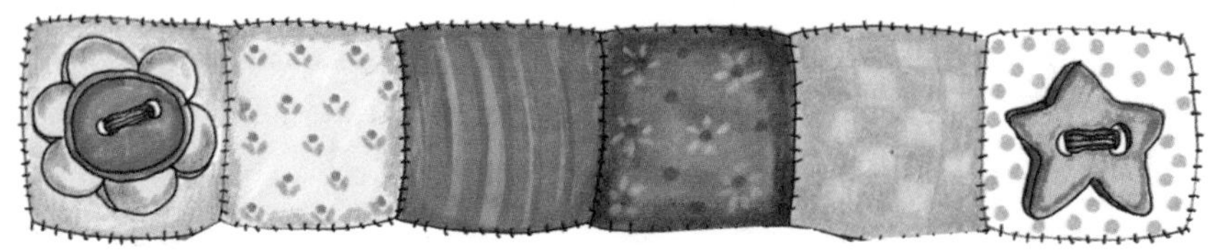

Dear God,

Thank you for my new baby sister. Could you make her do something besides sleep and cry? She's not much fun, maybe a kitten would be better.

Amen

I love You!
Welcome Home Baby Sister

Dear God,

My mom says that if you lined up all the little girls in the world and let her choose any one she wanted—tall or short, blond hair or black hair, freckles or not . . . she would choose me. I love my mom.

Amen

Dear Father,

I feel bad for my friend. Her dad got a new job in another state and they have to move. She's sad to leave her friends and her school and her church. I'm sad for her to go, too. I'll miss her lots. God, please help my friend to make new friends quickly in her new town. Help her to remember that you will still be with her at her new home. And that she has friends back here who won't forget her. Take care of her, God.

Amen

Dear God,

Please help my grandpa. He's very sick and I'm afraid he might die. I know that you can make sick people well. I've read about you doing that in the Bible. I feel better knowing that you are watching over my grandpa 'cause I know that you love him even more than I do. So, take care of him, God. Help him to remember how much you love him . . . and to remember that I love him, too!

Amen

Grandpa
Photos
Family
Photos

Dear God,

I hurt so bad. My Daddy moved out and I don't understand why. I miss him. I want things to be the way they used to be. Please take care of Daddy. Help him not to be lonely. Help him to remember that I love him very much. Don't let him forget me, God.

Amen

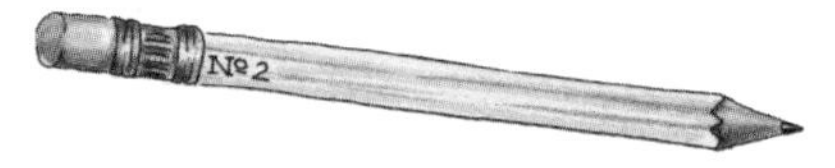

Dear Dad,
I miss
you. I wish

Dear God,

My heart is hurting. My grandpa died and I feel very sad. Grandpa could make me laugh even when I was grumpy and he taught me things like how to fish and how to make a birdhouse. Grandpa loved you so I know he's happy to be in heaven with you. Please God, take good care of my grandpa.

Amen

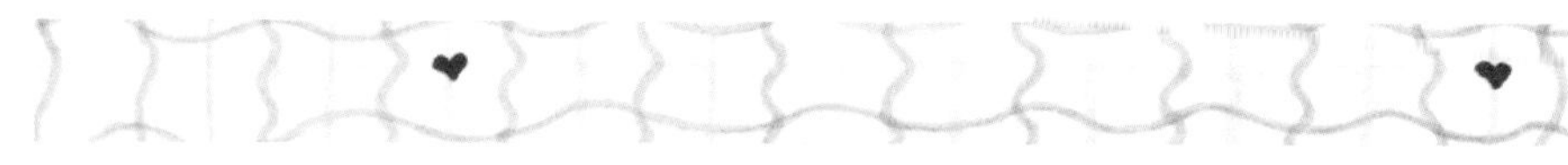

Tackle Box
I miss you Grandpa

Dear God,

I'm scared 'cause I have to do something hard today. I'm scared that I'm not smart enough. I've never done anything like this before. What if I don't do a good job? Will you help me when I ask you to? Please help me learn how to trust you. Thank you for hearing my prayer and thank you in advance for your help.

Amen

Please help me learn to trust you.
BIBLE

Dear God,

It's dark in here. There are some scary shadows on my wall. I think I heard a monster under the bed. I wish I had someone to hug. I know that you are here with me so I shouldn't be afraid, but I am a little. Could you snuggle in real close and stay with me all night? Thank you, God.

Amen

God is always with you

Dear God,

Can you hear the wind blowing? Do you see all the rain? You do remember your promise of no more big floods, don't you? The worst thing is the thunder and lightning. Why do storms have to be so noisy? I guess I'm kind of scared. Help me remember the pretty flowers and plants that will grow because of this storm. Help me think about rainbows after rain. Help me not be scared.

Amen

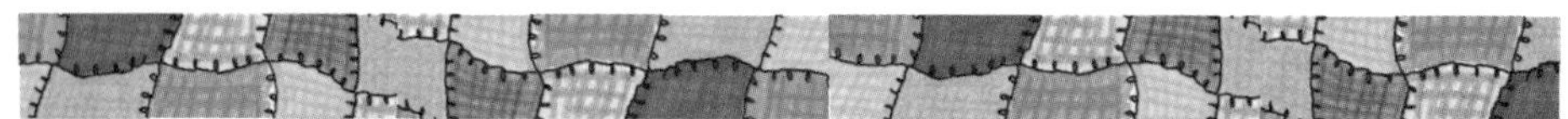

Dear God,

My friend is really sick. She might even die. That makes me feel bad. I'm glad that she loves you 'cause that means if she died, she would come to heaven with you. I would miss her though. Take care of my friend, God. And, God, if she does die, please don't let it hurt.

Amen

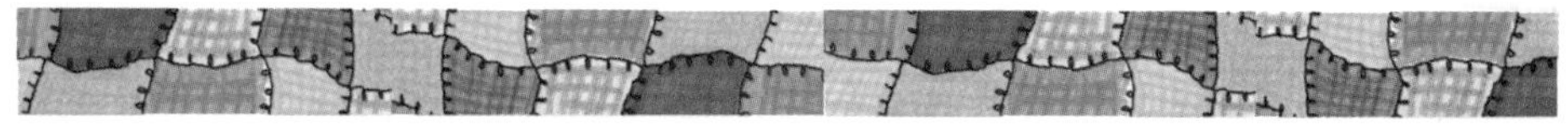

Dear God,

Who thought up book reports anyway? I have to stand up in front of my whole class and tell about the book I read. I'm scared that I'll forget what I want to say or that the other kids will laugh at me, or that I might even be sick in front of the whole class. Please help me, God. I read the book and I know what I want to say. Help me be calm and do a good job.

Amen

Book reports today
God is Great
A+ teacher

Dear God,

Everywhere I look I see moms and dads and kids all together—playing in the park or eating hamburgers in a restaurant. It makes me feel bad 'cause my mom and dad got a divorce. I miss us being all together. Help me understand, God. And help me remember that it's not my fault. Thanks for being there when I need to talk about it.

Amen

Dear Father,

My heart is hurting because my dog died today. He was the best dog in the whole world. Tramp was in our family before I was born. I loved playing tug-o-war with him and how he slept on the floor by my bed. I'm going to miss Tramp. Thanks for listening.

Amen

Tramp
Dear Tramp
I miss
You
very much
Tramp

Dear God,

My feelings are hurt. My friend told a lie about me to the other kids. They all laughed like it was really funny. I don't know why she did that. I want to hurt her back, but that isn't the right thing to do. Help me to forgive her and treat her with love.

Amen

SCHOOL

Dear God,

All the time my mom says that she loves me. That makes me feel good. 'Course I always know that she loves me but it sure feels good to hear it. Help me remember to tell people that I love them. Oh, and God, I love you.

Amen

Dear God,

I don't feel so good. My head hurts and my throat is scratchy. I don't like to be sick. I'd rather be outside playing with my friends. I know that you can help me feel better. Please help me to not be grumpy while I don't feel good. And help me to do everything my mom says to do so that I can feel better soon.

Amen

COLOR SET

Dear God,

My first gymnastics meet is tomorrow. I'm kinda scared. What if I forget my routines or what if I fall? I've practiced so hard and I really want to do well. Help me to be calm and to do the best I can do.

Amen

PRACTICE SCHEDULE
GIRLS A TEAM....
Mallory
Kelly
JoAnne
Shannon
Noelle
GIRLS B TEAM....
Hally
Caitlyn
Emily
over...
Gymnastics Meet
TODAY
2:00p.m.
Beam.. 2:30
Floor.. 3:30
Bars.. 4:30
Vault.. 5:30
Shoot for the stars....
23

Dear God,

Please help my mom and dad. They are always so busy—taking care of our house and yard, doing laundry, making food, doing stuff at church. But they still make time to play a game with me or read a book to me. Please take care of them and keep them healthy.

Amen

Bedtime
Stories
Bedtime

Dear God,

What a great day! I went to school and played with my friends and rode my bike and helped Mommy with dinner. I'm tired. I'm glad I can go to bed and get some rest now. Please keep me safe while I sleep and help me to get lots of rest so I have energy for tomorrow.

Amen

Jesus Loves
You
Mom's
Helper
Bike

Dear God,

Why do we have to move anyway? I like it here, this has always been my home. I like my house and my friends and my school. It's scary to move to a whole other town. Help me to remember that you will still be with me in our new town. Help me to make friends and to like my new school. It's scary, but it will be easier with you leading the way.

Amen

WELCOME to New Town
UP
Kitchen
Dishes
VILLAGE MAP
Moving Van
STOP

Dear Lord,

I have to go to the hospital to have my appendix out, whatever that is. I've never been in the hospital before. Help me to be brave, God. Help me to remember that you will be with me every minute. And God, could you make the doctor be really smart—so that he only takes out my appendix—not something else by accident.

Amen

HOSPITAL

Dear God,

Mom says that you
want me to love everyone.
Do you know my brother?
If you want me to love him
you'd better help me.

Amen

Toy

Dear God,

Why do there have to be wars anyway? Why can't everyone just share and get along? That's what my friends and I do and we hardly ever fight.

Amen

Dear God,

Did you really make the water in the Red Sea divide into two big walls? It would be cool if you did that in my bathtub . . . I don't really like taking baths. No, huh? Anyway, it's a great story about how you take care of your people.

Amen

Dear God,

Mom says I should be kind to others like the golden rule says, "Do unto others as you would have them do unto you." Most of the time I can do that just fine, but that girl down the street is hard to be kind to. Would you please give me an extra helping of kindness just to use on her? Thanks.

Amen

Dear God,

Why do people have to die? I'm sad because someone I love died. Mom says that person is with you in heaven now. I know that is good, but I still wish he was here with us. I'm glad we can all be together in heaven someday.

Amen

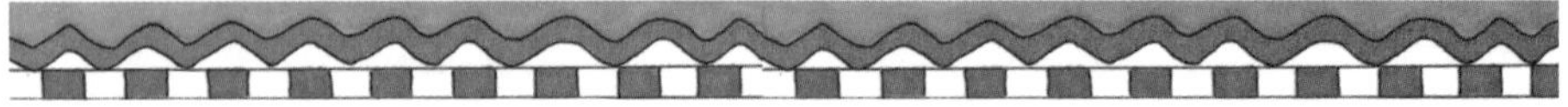

Dear God,

Tonight Mommy read me stories about Jesus. I like Jesus, he is really nice. He loves people, even people that no one else likes. And he helps people anytime he can. He's friendly and kind. I would like to be kind and friendly to everyone. Please help me be more like Jesus.

Amen

Little Girls Bible Storybook
Little Girls
Mothers